73

Dreamer

Books by Primus St. John

Skins on the Earth
Love Is Not a Consolation; It Is a Light
Dreamer

Dreamer

poems by

Primus St. John

Carnegie Mellon University Press
Pittsburgh 1990

ACKNOWLEDGMENTS

Portions of this work were published previously in *Callaloo, Rio Grande Review,* and *The Oregonian.*

Library of Congress Catalog Card Number 89-61326
ISBN 0-88748-097-7 (pbk.)
Copyright © 1990 by Primus St. John
Printed and bound in the United States of America
First Edition

Publication of this book is supported by a grant from the Pennsylvania Council on the Arts.

CONTENTS

Introduction

Dreamer is a remarkable book which readers may readily discover for themselves; however, because it differs in some ways from the current idea of a collection of poetry a few introductory remarks might be useful. Most recent books of poetry seem to bear a strong family resemblance, like cousins perhaps—they bring together one or two-page lyrics written in a more or less common idiom about everyday life. Now this is all well and good but it is only our age's idea of a book of poems just as a collection from another age might include a "Preface to Lyrical Ballads" or an elaborate and obsequious dedication to a patron. In short, any age's conventional ideas have their limits, limits which for our period are pointed up by Primus St. John's book, a book that doesn't fit the current stereotype. It is after bigger game.

St. John spent several months in 1984-85 in Barbados and *Dreamer* is what he returned with. It was hard to come by and therefore some effort is expected of the reader. Terms are used, for example, that are unfamiliar to most North American readers. To clarify such details notes have been provided at the end of the book.

Dreamer is about slavery but it is also about language, art, and the effort of creating a life in a world battered into being by slavery. In its deep concern with language this book works hard with the essentials of poetry—rhythm and imagery—in what seems to me to be a nearly elemental way, subtle as it is. The result is poetry of a very high order. But at its core is slavery in all its most despicable aspects: The Middle Passage, treated in an astonishingly new way, as well as the residual effects of slavery—the patronizing attitude toward African art for one thing—in addition to the unrelenting effect of slavery on the present. While reading this book we are faced with the unresolved and convoluted evil of slavery while also gaining a vision of the heroic efforts of generations of people in trying to find an identity and a language in the face of that evil.

Now these are large claims but *Dreamer*, I feel, bears them out. For instance, in the first section St. John deliberately contrasts the "sophisticated" language of a contemporary critic of African art with the voice of the original artist. This juxtaposition points up the inevitable gap between criticism and art while also revealing the everyday racism practiced by Western critics of African art. This of course is also one of the residual effects of slavery but one rarely singled out. In the voices of the artists the fact of slavery is also

7

always present in this section, but for me the key lies in those contrasting languages—the vitality and richness of the artists' words call into question at every turn the critic's racist and obtusely formalist remarks.

The strategy St. John uses to write about The Middle Passage—in Part II—is brilliant in its evocation of the life of John Newton who, after serving as a slave ship captain, became an Anglican priest and the author of that marvelous hymn, "Amazing Grace" as well as, and most notably, an abolitionist. To focus on Newton is a master-stroke which takes the reader inside the fevered and guilt-ridden mind of the slaver. By drawing on Newton's logs St. John keeps at his concern with language as a source of identity and power, themes which are further explored in Part III, the setting of which is contemporary Barbados. The present is permeated with the oppress effects of slavery, effects shown here in the hard search for union, identity, and a language, those essential qualities of life that were torn away from all slaves and which no emancipation gave back.

Dreamer is an important contribution to our culture and it is a privilege to be asked to introduce it to you. And, finally, my intro-duction is simply that: Here, reader, is *Dreamer*.

Vern Rutsala
Portland 1990

I

*"Mi wan' opodron
Lek friman borgu"*

"I want the drumming in the open
Like a citizen who is free."

"Fictive kinship ties probably resulted from
relationships among those who had been
on board slave ships together from West Africa."

We came to know each other
Through the constant touch of our bodies
The endless devotion
of our mingled sweat;
Finally I said,
"You stink," in my language
"Yoruba man, son of a Lagos beast,
So do you," he said
In his own language.
Almighty God, Olofin - Orun,
Discerner of hearts,
I did not kill him;
It was good to know
He too was still human,
For we have come to live
In the enormous hole
Of a world that creaks,
That rocks from side to side
Like the astonishing breast
Of the full moon.
A world fertile with death,
Seductive with madness,
With enough pain to produce crops;
And in this world
We have become as rancid
As salt fish after an enormous journey,
Rancid
With stories of enigmatic love
And profuse loss—
So Olorun
It was because we sensed
We were some last precious gift
For some lost future kin,
It was in that spirit
Wattled and daubed in our own shit
That we reached into the darkness
And became brothers.

*"In certain cases the ties may have
been more than 'fictive', since individual
cargoes certainly included captives from
common regions, villages and even families . . ."*

That day
The sun was especially hot;
I want to caution you
It may have unraveled my mind.
That day a Limba woman jumped.
"No matter what others believe," she said,
"I trust my own wisdom
And choose the enduring sea."
I too was at the edge;
A stench was upon us
As thick as soup.
The day before that
I was put down beside her
With the treacherous Wolof.
She had a thick crust of blood
Around her thighs,
Trickles of blood down her legs,
I admit she stank,
I wanted to dream my way into it.
I wanted to dream my way into it
Like gourds of cold sea water,
I wanted to seep my way
Into her darkness,
For ever since we were children
She has been as black
As the river at night to me.
We are from the same village;
Her father, chief.
She has been taught to ignore me;
She is so damn beautiful
And good at it
So damn beautiful
So quiet and peacefully black
And aloof
Beside her I am but a stalk
of dry grass in the harmattan.
That day

When they took us up on deck,
We all crumpled in the light
Spoke to ourselves
With the same crisp mockery
Of the snapping sails,
But not her.
I would have done anything
To clean her body.
Killed a hundred Wolof,
Turned into tears.
Swelled into a water gourd.
Transformed myself into goats
Or pigs and licked or chewed- -
For love is neither slavery
Nor grace nor cleanliness,
But an immense fire at the hearth
A tribal sacrifice
A curious self revelation
A lusty redemption
An unconditional desire
To be swept up with somebody
Into something else.
Someday
Before we are through in this house
From which I am afraid
We will never walk out alive,
I want to be shackled to her,
I want us to speak to each other
With the whole mouth.

"There are two ways of looking at African
Negro sculpture that, for fifty years, have impeded
a true understanding of that art. One
is the notion, that an African carving or casting
is 'pure art' and that its quality can be
fully possessed by European aesthetic standards,
without reference to the culture in and for
which it was made, the other and opposite
view sees in an example of Negro sculpture not
a work of art but merely a primitive utilitarian
object made by a tradition-fettered artisan
for a barbarous community devoid of aesthetic
feeling of any kind."

When the butterflies appear
The tilling of the fields begin.
We dance like shrill sounds
As light as we can
For creatures without wings
To the "do" spirits,
Looking at the world
through the veil of our painted mask
And braided ropes,
Hoping to imbue in ourselves
What we know in the soft earth
Is truly divine.

"... In 1934 no fewer than seven hundred and sixty
five stone [figures] and heads were discovered in
a clearing ... in a majority of these carvings
the features are sufficiently individualized for
them to be considered as portraits."

Today
I am working on the head of Osisi
The ambitious woman.

> My head — which is wearing
> a bright scarf today—
> Will surely give me
> male and female children.

It is as though I am working
On a silk cotton tree
In the forest.
Or an eagle in the sky,
Ambition, like death,
Is so demanding—
A little bush becomes a court case—
Yet
When I put my chisel in her face
I look for her in vain,
I must consult the oracle
To make the stone pregnant.

Keba,
A man of middle age,
Of sweet belly laughter,
Will be next.
People
Cannot run away from him.
He has a heart
the size of the chief's house.
I must keep the calabash
Full with wine
And the sun at his back.

Had I known my destination
Was to reach for heaven
From earth

15

through the indelible lines
and curves
Of what we are thinking
And who we are,
I would have asked
To be like the unanointed men
Who leave their lives behind
Like the birds
While their bodies take them
To other limbs.
But what I am ordained to do,
Is a hunters song,
An Ijala.

"For all this, however, we must still face the
fact that our knowledge of the background of
African art is elementary. And while we keep
in mind the vital importance of enriching,
whenever possible, the communication of a piece
of Negro sculpture through the marriage of
ethnographic and aesthetic considerations, we
should not quixotically deny ourselves the
aesthetic gratification which art is able
to provide each new generation of observers,
foreign as that gratification may be to the
essential character and message of Negro art."

I think I will make the man thin
Like my cousin Yerema
With the long neck.
He is ones self
In ones own right
A strong dark wood
As distinguishable from others
As a Mohammedian's sermon.
It will take three days
To sharpen my wits
and rough out the body.
I think I will make Zala
The woman.
She alone has the lips
Of early morning;
The enormous ability to fill and rise,
To gird herself in the loin cloth
Of your deepest thoughts
And understand them—
For this sculpture will be
The undergarment
For a couple in love,
And if you cut off
Any piece of it,
That piece will also grow.
And I will tell the wood
To tell the man inside
Kneel down on the ground
By his yams,

Then arch his back
And extend his long neck,
His face looking behind him.
And I will tell the wood
To tell the woman
Standing up behind him
To bend down
And kiss his lips,
Zala's breast,
Oh Zala
The perfect headrest.
And this pose
Will almost be a complete circle
Without hesitation or fear,
Not a place for a jealous man
Or an oppressed woman.
And the tension will be
Gentle and firm,
Held together by hunger
And appetite,
By chance and wisdom.
And you will see
How their loins burn—
After all who can escape
The small bearded gods
We worship . . .

This will be a piece that comes alive
And serves when lovers weep at night.

"On the northern shore of the Gulf of Guinea
especially in the Gold Coast and Ivory Coast, we
find a curious expression of lyric fantasy in
small bronzes produced by the cireplerdue
method and used by the natives for weighing
gold dust."

I told her to go outside
Little girl
Who is the younger of twins
And look carefully
At the small yellow birds
And to learn how to speak
With understanding of another,
For in this world
It is too easy to be a slave . . .

This was to be only a small piece
To weigh gold,
But later that afternoon
When she left
I also started to cut
The story into a large stone.
Of all that I saw them do
Only this song will be left out:

"I shall return no more, I shall return no more my [mother] "

I was to become a Bajan.
I did not know that;
I am a Wolof
Captured at the hoofs of my prey.
My name means
Fruit, seed, kernal.
I am my mother's
Youngest child;
I have never seen her again.
Never seen her mash or kneed
Or dip into the water again
To splash my face.
She was blunt,
And as stubborn as the beard
I hate to shave.
She was so beautiful
Tne village thought she was cursed.
She was so imperfect and warm
In her thoughts like an old fire .
Before I left I heard her say:

We call the dead — they answer
We call the living — they do not .

*"We judge a work of art by its effect on
our sincere and vital emotion, and nothing
else. All this critical twiddle-twaddle
about style and form, all this pseudo-
scientific classifying and analysing of books
in an imitation - botanical fashion, is
mere impertinence and mostly dull jargon."*

What do stories do?
Affect us,
Nothing else.
If that is scientific, fine;
If that is not, tough "T",
Twiddle - twaddle
And all that rot.
My response to the story
About the pig being slaughtered
Was like the eleven year olds.
"It made me sick."
Especially that part
When the knife dove into the throat,
Splash.
My legs went to jelly.
My head to peanut butter.
I thought it was cruel,
But I was moved
Like the blood gushing down,
To understand the need for food,
The need for trade
And the need to make families
Slaves.
Who was I to intervene or recoil
From the story.
It made me furious.
I kept thinking of all the blood
In the bucket
That holds names:
Akam — The small
Remnant of a once mighty people,
Sekyere with the capital
Dwaben to the east,
Kumase — a town,

Krobò — a mountain country.
I began to think of the dance
Asáw
In the blood,
The kindness — *ayam yé,*
Our sins and our worth,
The blood all over the language.
Osékám twà adé
(A knife cuts.)
Okromfó wi áde.
(A thief steals.)
Owo ka onípa.
(A serpent bites.)
In a story, I get involved.
I try to make the last page last.
I rivet myself to the names:
Kwasi, Abene, Benada
Kofi, Ata — a twin.
She always went there;
She was always told
Not to go.
Whereas I was blind
Now I see . . .
The blood in our language.
Mepe hó mmòn sènhá
(I like that place better than this,)
(I shall be able to match
Or to overcome him)
Metumi no,
(He is unequal to the business)
Otumí sa yò,
I am astonished,
Shocked,
I shudder at this story.
Boys were suddenly changed into fathers;
Fathers weeping became sons.
My head aches
As if the smith is still
Hammering iron,
Or the women giving birth.
I know
Like the pig in the story

People uttered groans,
The eloquent delivered speeches,
The militants foamed.
The earth produces food
In this story—
Lots of food . . .
Whereas I was blind
Now I can see.
A knife cuts.
A thief steals.

But reader,
What about you?

II

"As I said earlier, in imposing a conception on events, all human individuals create the 'reality' to which they respond"

Dreamer

There are few probabilities through
Which dreamers do not pass. . . .

The first dream
Is the bright red dream
Of our mother's heart.
It is her sacrifice
Of something eternal
In herself, for us.
The Arabs say
Blood has flowed
Let us begin again.

The heart is like a cup, or a coffer,
or a cave. It holds the image of the
sun within us. It is a center of illumination
and happiness and wisdom. To dream
of the heart is always to dream of
the importance of love. . . .

The second dream is the inauguration
of the soul. In this dream we are
confronted by a host of birds. . . .

Some were guiless
Like the doves,
said Odo of Tusculum,
Cunning
Like the partridges.
Some came to the hand
Like the hawks.
Others fled from it
Like the hens,
Some enjoyed the company
Of people
Like swallows,
Others preferred solitude
Like the turtle doves,
But all eventually flew away.

"Living is not necessary, but navigation
is," said Pompey the Great.

b, 1725, London
Mother devout as gun powder
Seemingly clairvoyant
Taught her only child
To read by four
Arithmetic and Latin by six
Dies when he is seven.

I am dreaming
I am in the dark
And it is raining
And she is the rain.

To dream that you are in the dark
is a sign of difficulties ahead; if
you fall or hurt yourself you can expect
a change for the worse, but if you
succeed in groping to the light that
is another matter. . . .

Father, master of ships,
Lively in the Mediterranean trade,
Unusual qualities—
Educated in Spain, stern.

I listen to nothing
But the silence
Of my father; the dream
Says
He is the rudder
And the compass.

If, in your dreams, you see your
father and he speaks to you, it is
a sign of coming happiness. If he is
silent, or if he appears to be ill or
dead, then you may expect trouble. . . .

Sent to sea at ten,
Acted like a verb in disagreement,
Of course
Bright,
But no eagle—
A mess.

I have vague
Dreams now
Of intelligent flowers.
I cannot say
If their roots
Are in the ground
Or in the air.

By seventeen
A wild flower
In the field of Jesus.
Pious, books, fasting,
Abstinence from meat,
A canon in his meditation
And silence,
But like the weeds
Loved to curse.

Flowers, one of nature's best dreams.
This foretells great happiness, unless
you throw away the blossoms. . . .

1742
A lot more flexible,
Falls in love,
Misses his ship,
A free thinker now,
Less of a thorn
In the side of God.

I dream that I
Am always with her,
A freckle on her wrist,
A flower in her hair,

29

A ridiculous flying fish—
Sliced
And dressed
And set on the table.

As I told you before,
He missed his ship,
Became a lover
Rather than a Jamaican
Planter,
Father as expected
Furious.

Love is a dream of contraries as far
as sweethearts are concerned. To dream
that you do not succeed in love is a
sign that you will marry and have
a happy life. To dream that you are in
the company of your lover is also fortunate. . . .

Late 1743
Kidnapped into the Navy
(What else)
Coming from Mary's house,
Taken from his own life
Focused into new pieces.

I dream about my fortune,
A fragrance captured
In a jar,
A freckle without a wrist,
A wisp
Fox like at the edge
Of the wind.

Fortune is a dream of contraries: The more
fortunate and successful you are in imagination
the greater will be your real struggles . . . .

How do we fit together
When we are not free?
What kind of animal are we?
How many heads do we have ?

How many tails?
The sea
Is a strange piece of property
On which to discuss this,

On the HMS Hardwick
One month later
Midshipman John Newton:

I have eaten war
Like a cluster
Of delicious fruit.
The ironic juices
Running from my lips
That was my dream.

The reality of war is the dream of it. Beware
of those things that appear so friendly
but have no reason. . . .

1774
The Hardwick
Ordered to the East Indies.
First our hero visits Mary again.
(Your wrong)
Almost misses ship,
Completely misses the point.
Given small boat of men
To go ashore at Plymouth,
Deserts.

My dreams here
Were father, compass,
fog, leakage ,
And ultimately, learning,
With us
Like our laundry.

We are always pulling from our past. Fossils
are the dream of the sickness of someone
you have not met for a long time. When
this happens brew herbs, add honey

and lemon, sip and inhale deeply. . . .

Captured like a frog,
Returned, put in irons,
Stripped, flogged, degraded,
Returned to formast.

This is that point many people would
call a black moment, an unfortunate
color on things. I will not do that. For
black is a contrary at funerals and our
hero has just died a little as we
all tend to from time to time. And even
though that is true I will not do
that either. I will not talk of the great
white moment of death, I will not talk
of the great blue and purple moments
in the prosperity of pain. I will not
talk of the great red or scarlet moments
of quarrels and loss of friends, or
the crimson pleasure of the unexpected,
the mental tints of yellow and orange
that show you should always expect
change, or the feeling of knowing Green
because you have been on a long journey.
All the colors are conjurors when our
mysteries are being solved. And if this could
not be his dream then by now it should
be ours. . . .

We are not holy
The wind says in the sails
As he works.
It has never been otherwise
Though we live in the most
Devout of stories like litmus paper
Constantly changing color
Just to prove something
is happening.

The sadness in his dream is a good omen
for the future. It is a quest for lasting joy,

and so is punishment a dream of unexpected
pleasure. . . .

Works quietly for weeks.
His silence
Darns a temperate
Healing thread.
His eyes
Become an elaborate
Decorative art
Avoiding everyone.

Every month, said Cicero
The moon contemplates
Its trajectory
And the shrubs
And animals grow.

He has done to himself
What is easy.
He must now blossom
Out of his new secrets
Even if joy is ephemeral.

Suddenly
He begins to sing,
Creates songs about fish
And clouds.

Fish are a dream of penetrative motion,
Clouds are a dream of appearances always
in a state of change. . . .

We must be patient
With the over-fecundity
Of his youth.
We must let him
Climb and descend the mast
Like a weapon.
Trade him
To a slavers ship
To subdue the threat

To discipline
In his strangely awakening
Joy.
We must let him
Choose his monsters
And the myths
Of his own worth—
The enemy always being
The forces threatening
From within.

Paul said, "We wrestle not against flesh
and blood, but against principalities, against
powers, against the rulers of the darkness
of this world, against spiritual wickedness in
high places. . . ."

Suddenly,
Begins to breathe
Different songs
In his six months stay
Along the Sierra Leone coast.
Troublesome songs,
Songs of quick wit
And devastating rhymes
Ridiculing ship's officers,
Crew loves them,
Becomes a choir.

To dream that you hear other people
singing shows that the difficulties
that will come for you will come through
your dealings with other people. . . .

The irrate mate
Assuming command
After the death of the captain
Threatens
To put Newton
On a man-of-war.

The royal navy is not an obstacle dream;
it is an elaborate exhibition of the
nuances of living death. . . .
Occupation: slave dealer
Place: Sierra Leone
On one of the Plantanes
Features: Short, white male
Name: Clow
Other information: black wife
Name: sounds like P.I.

John Newton
Bargains his life
Into this extravagant story.
He will become a slave
Because P.I. will hate him.
He will become ill
With fever.
He will be denied
Food,
Denied water,
Tormented by black slaves
On command,
Put to work
On a lime tree plantation
Enjoying only the scents
And dreaming
Of his earthly desires
Will master the six books
Of Euclid,
Drawing the diagrams
With a long stick
In the wet sand.

Six is like *two* a particularly ambiguous
number to dream about, but it
establishes equilibrium. It unifies
the triangles of fire and water and
symbolizes the human soul. Six is
the hermaphrodite, a personality integrated
despite its duallty.

If this is a story
Of the reasoning of slavery,
Where are we?
What have we been doing
To people,
To the light
From which life emanates?

Slavery is a story
Of procreation,
Of magic religious thinking,
Of the androgynous divinity
within us.
No story can be this happy
Unless it is married
To something deeply within us.
It is not *them*
Who have done it to *us*,
Or *us*
Who have done it to *them*.
It is the antagonistic dream
Of unreconciled love.

To dream of erotic love is to dream of
the desire to die in the object of desire, to
dissolve in that which is already
dissolved. The Book of Baruch says erotic
desire and its satisfaction is the key
to the origin of the world. Disappointment
in love and the revenge which follows
in its wake are the roots of all the evil
and selfishness in the world. The whole
of history is the work of love.

II
"The character of the image," says Shukrâshârya,
"is determined by the relationship between
the worshipper and the worshipped."

On the beach,
He eats the fruit
Of his own way;
He fills himself
With his own devices;
He continues to draw
In the sand.

Each grain
Is a small,
Precise form
Of salvation
That has occurred,
A god come to earth
In another form,
A private,
Innate sacrifice.
Providence does not tire.
We are ready to go on
With the story.

It has come to this:
When his father dreams
He only sees
The broad face
Of sadness,
The soft grassland
Where only asphodels grow,
And the idea of water
Expanding into tears.

But to dream of sadness is a good
omen, a transposition of suffering to the
spiritual: This dream is like an herb,
a seasoning, a bitter root, medicinal,
sometimes poisonous, but never-the-less
something that eventually withers away.

When you
Come on to squally weather,
When the wind
Is about SW,
When
You sway up the yard,
Fix the try sail,
Put people to making
Sinnet and swab,
Ask for my son .
Ask the *lamb*,
The *Beverly*, the *Golden Lyon*,
Ask Job Lewis
Have you seen my boy?
Have you seen my boy?

One thousand years before Christ, Solomon
said that the way of a ship in the midst
of the sea was too wonderful for him
to understand.

Meanwhile,
Clow: shamed
Into freeing his fellow
Whiteman.
After all
They share the same hair,
The same instinctual life,
The same irrational power.
There is no victim here:
This is a story of love's
Sadness,
Of the spirit of love's ferocity
And savage insensibility,
And the name of Jesus
Turned in hymns,
Spewed into the fringes
Of the forest,
Spewed on the deep blue sea.

What dream is this, is that what you said?
My God, this is the dream of the dragon,

the fabulous animal, the amalgam of
aggression, the serpent, the crocodile, the
lion, what we like to think is the
antediluvian nature of love.

John is free now.
John is free to slave,
Free to be reluctant,
To give up profit
And return home.

Ask the master of the Greyhound.
Have you seen my boy?
Have you seen my boy?

To find money in your dream is not fortunate
at all. There will be some sudden advancement
or success, but it will prove
disappointing. Reader, remember this
statement by Virgil, "It will be pleasant
to remember these things hereafter."

You cannot blame
The sea on a woman.
Unlike the seasons
It has no ribs
Though
It has a crown,
Wears a sheaf,
Swings a sickle,
Adores the sun,
And is known
As bare headed and leafless.
The sea is the emblem
Of the great capricous world;
The naked image of flux
Vibrating between life and death.

There is a dream called "dire is the tossing
deep the groans; come let us heel, list
and stoop." And when John heard this
On his way home, it was as if he

had read II Kings 10:16 "Come with me
[brother] and see my zeal for the Lord . . ."

For twelve months
The *Greyhound*
Sought gold,
Ivory, dyer's wood,
Bees wax,
And Newton sought the Lord.

The way of a ship in the midst of the sea
is too wonderful to understand.

Youth is not innocence.
It is not a militant puzzlement.
It is a methodical initiation
Into the ubiquitous life
Of sin.
For a life without sin
Is no life at all.
And so he wanders on
Like Paul,
So very christian about it,
At once wretched and delivered.
Thinking with his mind
He is serving God,
But with his flesh
The law of sin.

Call out John Newton.
Call out
To Joshua, Ruth,
Samuel, Obadiah,
Esther, Zachariah,
Luke and Timothy.
The world
Is a masterfully round
Secret
That embraces everything,
And it is time
To reach into the horizon,

Now.
It is time to choose
Your ship,
And the triangle of your life
upon the salty sea.

As you can see, dreams are without reason,
without solution, without proof, the
unedited version of our love, our aspiration,
our hurt . . . Call out John Newton. Call out. . . .

Back home
Offered captaincy of ship.
Refuses.
Sails as first mate
On the Brownlow.
Collects slaves.
Takes them to South Carolina.

He begins the dream of question: "What
was the mode used in stowing the slaves
in their apartments?"

Returns home,
Marries Mary Cattlett,
Assumes first command,
The Duke of Argyle,
140 tons burthen.

Marriage is the dream of sulphur and
mercury. Some believe it is a most fortunate
omen, a volatile conciliation, a fragile
union. They are right. It is one of the great
uncharted seas of individuation. It is
said, "If you are separated from your
opposite you consume yourself away. . . ."

Dead reckonings
Magnetical Amplitude   W° 25.30N°
True Amplitude   W° 6.30
Variation   19° in Western
Lattitude per Account   50° 48^m

1/3 of the slaves will die
In middle passage
Some say fifty million
Started the trip
Some say fifteen.

The dream of questions is a bright necklace
with two ornaments on it: liberty and
love, not truth.

"At noon some small rain. . .
Had an indifferent observation . . ."

"We take the two men boys
For some shallop rigging,
We do not take
The two fallen breasted women. . ."

"Dear Mary,
    Today, saw
    My quondam black
    Mistress P.I. -
    I believe
    I made her sorry
    For her former ill
    Treatment of me."

The trouble with atonement is it is like
a sphinx, several parts human, several
parts bull, dog, lion, dragon or bird.
When we are dreaming of atonement, no
matter how subtlely, we must remember
we are not dreaming of a verb.

"I watch them work
The tie, tackle,
And lower lift.
The Boatswain
Speaks to Bredson
About the score
In one of the strops.

Thomas Creed
Sits with his splicing fids;
Tucks the strands
Of the tack cringle.
His fingers are either
Little mystics or snakes."

When you dream the dream of square sail
rigging you are dreaming the dream
that the same side is always before
the wind. At the dawn of Swedish History
it was believed Erik Vaderhall, the
King of the Sveas, could turn the wind
and cruise endlessly. Ships are suppose
to be emblems of transcendental joy. . . .

"Do the male slaves
Ever dance
Under these circumstances?"

"After every meal
They are made to jump
In their irons;
But I cannot call it dancing."

"What is the term
That is usually given to it?"

"It is by the Slave dealers
Called dancing."

"Unclewed the sails,"
They too in their shackles
Danced in the wind."

"Dear Mary,
    I watched the land wind
    Do to the sails
    What it does
     To our hair.
    I dreamed of dancing
    With you

Into the cold water,
Our wet clothes
Like nets and entanglements
Around our desire."

They would call them up
two by two, equivocal,
Unmasked,
Making it possible
To be classified
Forever:
Pairs of birds,
Pairs of oxen,
Pairs of sheep,
Reptiles, lions,
Elephants, antediluvian,
Carnivorous, herbivorous,
Fabulous, beautiful,
Ugly, strange,
Cocks, locust,bears,
Foxes and even flies,
All of them black;
All of them in colonnade
To the gates of hell.

John did baptize
In the wilderness,
Did call out to Judaea
And Jerusalem
Come lay down
Your life
In the River Jordan,
Participate in his death
And his resurrection.

They said
They were refreshing them,
But the shackles still clanged,
And most of them still stank,
And many finding holes
In the netting
Jumped overboard

And baptized themselves
Bobbing in the adoring
Loins of the sea.

"Dear Mary,
    The three greatest blessings
    Of which human nature is capable
    Are undoubtedly religion,
    Liberty and love."

The shape of a ship's hull is determined by
the materials, methods of construction,
means of propulsion, use, fashion, and
whim. This is a dream of law and
the minute verities of justice the 8th
enigma of the Tarot.

First part fair,
The latter cloudy,
Winds becoming unusual,
Clouds dark, great lightning . . .

I think of what we've done,
My own illumination
Before it is too late:

The palm and needle whippings,
The short splice,
Blackwail hitches
Sheet bends.

Quickly rummage
The rigging details,
The yardarm blocks,
The tackles.

Recall work
On the pintles
The rudder head.

Have Billinge
Check barricado and stores

Especially powder and slaves.

On this day
Of the second voyage
Of *The African*, 1754,
Weighed,
Bound by God's permission
To St. Christophers,
We are ready for our justice,
To be winnowed like barely
On the threshing floor.

The great dream of the dark, with the
lonely extroverted lamp, the intuitive ship
and the wind tossing on the innovative sea
should moor somewhere. "Why is this
so," asked Kuo Hsi. For in our landscapes
and our seascapes are the personalized items
of our consciousness, the course grist
of our imagination, the flirtatious metaphors
stirring our ethics, and the boldly stroked
delineations of our unraveling possibilities
and original nature.

Through the night
We were played with
Like kittens.
The slaves spilled
Out nightmares of themselves
And groans.
We will all
Need dawns shawl
This morning.
I hope
She is good to us.

Osiris was slain by Set and put
together again by Isis. John will dream
like this, off and on, and then quit the
sea. This is his last voyage. He will
lose no slaves and no crew, and it will
be called a blessing. At a time like

this the Egyptians would build a
monolith to marry the enigmatic tension
between life and death. John will
change his dreams, now, from the menstrual
dreams of the slaver to the menthol dreams
of the minister. Showing the devastating evil
we do, like a storm, is only a stepping
stone to something else.
Sing brother.

I will become sermons,
He says,
That understand what I've done .
Sing
I will become hymns
Bound in the skin
Of what I've done.
I will be patient with Cowper,
Inspiring to Wilberforce
    and Wordsworth;
I will attract the awaken crowds,
The abolitionist.
I will stand at the alter.
Sing brother
Dressed in black,
Testifying,
Testifying . . .

I dream I will not be forgiving him
for the timeliness of his innocence, for
betrothing the dead to the dead, but lifting
up my hands to an appetite for life
that will take slavers and slaves with me.

I wish
There was no timelessness,
That slavery was over
And so far away
It was an incredibly mysterious
Jungle—
Somewhere else.
An uncharted river

Canopied by extensive moss—
Somewhere else.
A spectacular ragged
Waterfall
Mystically expressed
Over an enormous
Obsidian wall,
But it is *right here*
In my pouch, today,
Like the acori beads
I have been swimming with
For hours—
Presidential, prime ministerial,
Corporate, grass roots based.
Right here,
Racist, imperial and sexist.
Right here,
Woefully spend thrift
and democratic,
Anally retentive
and republican,
Militantly inappropriate,
And so good to itself
That it jogs.

III

"Monkey say wha' in him mout, no fe him,
but wha' in him belly a fe him."

"What is in my cheek is not mine, but what has
gone into my belly that is my very own."

That In Itself Is The Proverb

Tonight
The old man sits outside the shack—
Buckpot moon, bad,
Unconscious,
Long unwithered hair
Shaking on the sea like dread locks.
He is quiet, unlike Babylon.
Quiet as the small gazelle
Or the strone, brutal leopard,
And black enough,
That in itself is the proverb.
Indeed, I hear the sea
Cus' at Bottom Bay
Say *phhh*, say *phhhh*
A little more human than before
Phhhh and *cus'*.

Gazelle man, quiet
Laid back like Jah.
Obviously, he loves she;
Secretly, he adores she butt—
Phhhh, *phhh*, and *cus*, *cus*
In Babylon.

I think, he would give her bare bananas
For her blue dress,
And behave in the spume about she
Like you have to grieve before you walk,
Like you have to mumble before you talk.
Old man, Egret . . .
Know she lips brackish.
Know she eyes merely Manchineels,
Know she against the cliffs,
Cus, *cus* and *phhhh*.

For a moment,
Caught up in your ethereal value
Not to move but to be,
I, too, feel old enough
To understand the sea.

Sunday

Today,
The sea has its own religion,
It is as blue
As an acori bead
I rubbed in my hand.

I think
Of swimming out
     for miles
          and miles
               in prayer.

I think
Of never struggling back
In doubt.

As though
In a world like this
Love starts over and over again.

We Are Going To Be Here Now

I wanted to start the story
In the hedge row
At the side of the road
Like the khus-khus grass.
You can be anyone you please.
If I can be Mr. Tambo.
Dig me out of the ground;
Hang me up
And when I'm dry
And fragrant,
And you're still wet,
You'll see that I can't
Live without you, baby,
My fishtail palm,
My cane,
My rondeletia.
And even in our games,
Hemped and flaxed in the imagination,
I believe you
Like I believe Olaudah Equiano,
Completely,
Tone and all,
And any of us who have been stolen
And runaway from the subscriber
With a cloth jacket
Or a thin dress.
Run into the hills to become cattle
Or horses, cimarroned,
And finally free—
Animals again.
God, I believe you history
Because your touch is a shore
Against the southern equatorial currents
Behind us,
And we are here now.
And at night when you embrace me
I know it is Antigua
Because Surinam is mortally ill—
Toal stand is doodstyk krankon.

We are going to be here now.
Here in the trusted word of the ground cover,
The worm weed
Used in the ritual bath after childbirth.
Here in the juice of the spanish needle
For our blind inflamed eyes.
We are going to be nivway,
And paw paw, and duppy-gun
Until our nails become the arrowheads
Of our profound loss,
And we offer them up again,
This time not as God and Gold
But as Race and Gender
Until we finally create America.

Lord, Man

You pick a basket of bean;
"God," you say,
When you mouth wide open
I see the wonderful round world.
I say, "Lord, man, you a beast,
You a beast."
I begin to feel my feet turn hoof.
You mouth, woman,
Turn sea grape, gully plum, dunks.
Hair on my arms turn weeds
Of the field:
Duckweed, sour grass, pussley,
From now on *burning mouth vine.*
Whatever we do or say,
Will smell like breath of earth,
Will be the soul giver of children,
Will curve like a weapon
Into terrible scars,
          I know
I will love you like a war,
And repent like medicine,
Almighty God, Imana,
The one who plans,
The protector of possessions,
Release me from your arms, now.
Never save me,
Let me love like thunder,
Let me grieve like famine,
Let me hurt her like I hurt the forest,
Let there be days
When it is wished all men were dead,
Because I done been through this already,
Because I done been through this already,
And it won't save the poem.

Tale

Cat gone down the road.

What she name, girl?
Jane (cat).

What happen to cat's tongue
I ask.
I got it she say.

What you name?
Jane, too.

You know what happen Jane (girl)
When you got cat's tongue?
No.

The language change

You see it (language)
Put its belly down and yawn.

That yawn makes the verbs quiver
Like cocks of lightning,
And lightning is a sign you know.
It can put a hole in the ground.

The mother of pots is a hole in the ground.
The mother of people is God.
The mother of language is that cat's tongue.

Tongue is a planter like hoe,
        a silence like seed,
        a consort like water.

What you say you name again?
Jane.
You gonna be busy girl.

Once

Once I went hunting in the bush
Of the human skull.

To please the people I met,
I gave flesh.

If by chance you happen to find me
And I am at rest,

It is their gift.

Worship

The storm god kneels down
And attends the river.
Men bring their boats in
With the same beat
That pumps their hearts.
When they are finished,
They stand in a huddle
And admire him.
Some think over the years
His hair has grown longer
And so magnificent
For the crowds that provide
The bones, and the blood,
And the breath of his life.

Focus

Riding through the sky
In a new chariot,
Dawn comes
With his ruddy horses,
His mother and his wife.
Rasta man wades
Into the full force of the sea
With him,
Letting the water meander
In his matted locks
And compose itself into tributaries
As he swims.
Knotty head man needs this moment
Of affirmation.
He too is a prince
Spilling out of the darkness.

And as he does so,
I reach for my stout black brethren,
My camera.
It is not as heavy as the false,
Or as intricate as loss.
I both focus and forsake,
Focus and forsake,
Like a man freed
From his own death,
Until I know it is right.
So Jah did it
And did not really die,
But went into himself.
And so *Rasta man* swims off,
Deeply into the God he is praying to.
And as he finally raises his hand
For the catch,

I click.

59

Talk

He hand on me back
Movin
Movin
Like a sentence
Assembling he words.

How he do this
Belong
To the many small bearded mysteries
Of the Lord they God
Moving on dis earth.

I know what you are doin
Maan.
Like the object of the verb,
I feel you slidin you hand
Down to me backyard
Like you own the whole daam house—

Sayin, "*woom - an, woom - an*
The night belong to we."

You are a fragrant politician:
Part marvelous *black sage*,
Part spotted *search me heart*,
Part *ganga* in de mind,
Fool,
Part *English lime*.
Barbados, the night belong to we,
Barbados, the beaches belong to we.

I see you
Like I see the natural process
Of weight and height;
A significance moving beyond me.

You an ol' man ya know;
Got more children
Than you got teet'.

What you think you gonna do
With me?

Yet you holding me
Nice na:
Like a garden *callaloo*,
An *ox eye daisy* or *a hug me close* . . .

Saying,
"*Dar - lin, Dar - lin*
Love don't love nobody but you."

Byum, you too *day*, man;
        you too *day*—
And precious,
Love.

When I am in the hands
Of the *Allhambys*
You give me the shirt off you
Back
And the blood in you heart.

You more than a village ram
On a walk;
You a touching man
Who talk start high
Off the ground in a large tree
And works its way down to the roots.

I use you words like baskets,
Ol' as I am.
I use you patience
Like seasoning on meat.

You know . . .
Love ain't using nobody,
Nobody but you.

Dread

It is simple, black man,
You must engage the unconscious.
Rastafari is in you.
The fierce symbol of the lion
Is love.

Dread locks, maan,
Knotty dread

It is your stark raving possibility,
It is your discontent,
And you are sanctified.
It is your denied self come closer,
And you are sanctified.
Rebel leader after rebel leader,
You are sanctified.
Slave revolt after slave revolt,
And you are sanctified.

Dread locks, maan
Knotty dread

It is that look in your eyes
When you're traveling back.
It is revival
By bits and pieces of the spirit
Possessed.
It is the pain of the absence
Become presence.
It is Africa.

So dread locks, maan,
Knotty dread,
The fierce symbol of the lion.
Is love.

Pearle's Poem

She sits in the marketplace
Issuing, like a bright star.
The origin of this beauty
Is her print dress,
So wild and deeply moving
It is a fable
By which to live,
To blend into
As if it were a mosaic of water
Coursing through Guyana
To the unreadable sea.
It has the lightning of her heart,
The thundering battles
Of her guilt and pain,
The dense jungles of her unrequited sorrow
Where the bright birds of her hope
Calypso into their ectasy.

In front of her
Is her biblical bondage
Of yams, breadfruit,
Mangoes and pears,
Each stacked like a seperate prayer,
A redeeming angel,
And the triumphant disposition
Of a true saint.
Women like her
Do not cry or laugh in public,
They condense
The antithetical flaws of the world
Into an awakened responsibility of color.
They are not imperialist
With an urgent knowledge;
They are people who doze in impudent hats
Who have remained
The intricately unravelled villagers

Of the themes of rain and sun
And draught
Part earth, part wind
And like my dying mother,
Part fire.

Pentecostal

All night
I kept my loneliness to myself
Like the wind god Amalivaca
Did for many years,
Then folded it up
Into the ends of the morning darkness
In small enough pieces
To blow through my four-hole flute.
I am looking for a cicle of dancers
Who touch
By the nature of their unusually
Long shadows,
I am looking for a drum beat
To accompany
What is a bloodknot of kindness
Between us,
Taken
From the great strength of a healing music,
Taken
From the sanctuary of a singer's open hands
That eventually
Will plait us into strands
Of the everlasting hair
That make up the forgiving rainbow.

Song

Fishermen
Pursue the sea
As if it were
A naked woman,
That is why
They rise early
And leave their wives
And go to boats
To mumble through
All the natural
Gradations of purpose
That are deeply imbued
In the incomprehensible
Pain of living.

Don't get me wrong,
The sea
Does not want them
At all
No matter what it's done,
And that is why
Ahab went mad
When he saw the sea
Is just what it is,
The sea,
And nothing more,
Despite the fine crepe dresses
The wind and sun
Love to wear.
And they in turn
Are not mendacious
At all
For how they behave,
For they are not human
Beings
Facing year after year
With the unwitting limits
Of surreal nets
And traps that work

Like threatening dreams.

They are just
Capricious things
Trying to feel comfortable
At what they do.
And despite all their seductivity,
The fishermen
Are able to find
In the essential qualities
Of the plain deep water itself
That source
For the silence in themselves,
For their ecstatic gasps of joy
And their pruned, unwilling
Sighs of loss.

And if that is not what love is for,
Then what is it?

Carnival

The sun's return is magical;
And once a year, finally
More than we can bear.
That is why, suddenly,
We break out into a sensual
Frenzy of light
And sound
And motion
And color
Plunging ourselves into chaos,
For we are nervous
But we say it is a celebration
As we realize our lives
Have been nothing more
Than a mischief of patterns
And organizations
Against our fear of the capricious —
Like the essence of the trees and caves,
Like the essence of the growing crops
Like the essence
Of all the herds of animals,
Like the essence of the clan and tribe,
Even our passionate anger,
Even our violence,
Even our cold indifference,
Our clandestine cruelty,
Our gentle warmth,
Our nurturing abundance,
And our generosity
As we struggle with our volatile selves
Trying to become one with the god's.

TEXTUAL NOTES

PART I

BAJAN - A Barbadian - one from Barbados.
HARMATTAN - A hot dry wind from North Africa.

IJALA - A hunting song - a song that deals with the epic struggles
and mythical issues present in the hunt.

LAGOS BEAST - An insulting name for a Yoruba man or woman.
LIMBA - A West African people.
OLOFIN-ORUN (also ORUN) - A Yoruba diety.

WOLOF - A West African people, disliked because they helped
European slavers raid for slaves.

PART II

"Dreamer" tells the story of John Newton, Anglican minister,
abolitionist and hymnist, known as the author of "Amazing Grace". He
was a slave ship captain before turning to the ministry. The poem
depends on a reading of his ships' journals and some biographical
essays.

PART III

ACORI BEAD - A small blue bead.

ALLHAMBYS - A family of money lenders in Barbados known for their
bizarre and ruthless methods of collecting.

AMALIVACA - A South American Indian diety.
BUCKPOT - A small ceramic cooking stove and pot.
CALLALOO - A wild grass used as greens.

CIMARRON - A Spanish word for runaway horses and cattle - later,
word becomes maroon - a runaway slave living in the
hills and forest.
 CUS - A contraction of "curse".
DREAD LOCKS - A matted hairstyle worn by RASTAFARIANS.

GANJA - Pot.
IMAN - An African diety.
JAH - God.
KHUS-KHUS GRASS - The hedgerow grass that grows along the edge of a sugar cane field - tall and thick.
KNOTTYHEAD MAN - Reference to Rastafarian dread locks.

MACHINEEL - A tree whose fruits are poisonous and will also cause skin irritation.

OLAUDAH EQUIANO - An 18th C African who wrote one of the earliest known slave autobiographies.

PAW PAW, DUPPY GUM, NIVWAY - Native West Indian plants.

RASTA MAN - A Rastafarlan, a religious group who believe Emperor Haile Selassie was God's human manifestation on earth, that the "new world" is a Babylonian captivity for black people. They have a strong committment to love and peace.

SEA GRAPES, GULLY PLUMS, DUNKS, DUCK WEED, SOUR GRASS, PUSSLEY - Some fruits and wild grasses.

MR. TAMBO - One of the characters in a minstrel show dialogue.

Carnegie Mellon University Press Poetry

1975
The Living and the Dead, Ann Hayes
In the Face of Descent, T. Alan Broughton
1976
The Week the Dirigible Came, Jay Meek
Full of Lust and Good Usage, Stephen Dunn
1977
How I Escaped from the Labyrinth and Other Poems, Philip Dacey
The Lady from the Dark Green Hills, Jim Hall
For Luck: Poems 1962-1977, H.L. Van Brunt
By the Wreckmaster's Cottage, Paula Rankin
1978
New & Selected Poems, James Bertolino
The Sun Fetcher, Michael Dennis Browne
A Circus of Needs, Stephen Dunn
The Crowd Inside, Elizabeth Libbey
1979
Paying Back the Sea, Philip Dow
Swimmer in the Rain, Robert Wallace
Far from Home, T. Alan Broughton
The Room Where Summer Ends, Peter Cooley
No Ordinary World, Mekeel McBride
1980
And the Man Who Was Traveling Never Got Home, H.L. Van Brunt
Drawing on the Walls, Jay Meek
The Yellow House on the Corner, Rita Dove
The 8-Step Grapevine, Dara Wier
The Mating Reflex, Jim Hall
1981
A Little Faith, John Skoyles
Augers, Paula Rankin
Walking Home from the Icehouse, Vern Rutsala
Work and Love, Stephen Dunn
The Rote Walker, Mark Jarman
Morocco Journal, Richard Harteis
Songs of a Returning Soul, Elizabeth Libbey
1982
The Granary, Kim R. Stafford
Calling the Dead, C.G. Hanzlicek
Dreams Before Sleep, T. Alan Broughton
Sorting It Out, Anne S. Perlman
Love Is Not a Consolation; It Is a Light, Primus St. John
1983
The Going Under of the Evening Land, Mekeel McBride
Museum, Rita Dove
Air and Salt, Eve Shelnutt
Nightseasons, Peter Cooley
1984
Falling from Stardom, Jonathan Holden
Miracle Mile, Ed Ochester

Girlfriends and Wives, Robert Wallace
Earthly Purposes, Jay Meek
Not Dancing, Stephen Dunn
The Man in the Middle, Gregory Djanikian
A Heart Out of This World, David James
All You Have in Common, Dara Wier
1985
Smoke from the Fires, Michael Dennis Browne
Full of Lust and Good Usage, Stephen Dunn (2nd edition)
Far and Away, Mark Jarman
Anniversary of the Air, Michael Waters
To the House Ghost, Paula Rankin
Midwinter Transport, Anne Bromley
1986
Seals in the Inner Harbor, Brendan Galvin
Thomas and Beulah, Rita Dove
Further Adventures With You, C.D. Wright
Fifteen to Infinity, Ruth Fainlight
False Statements, Jim Hall
When There Are No Secrets, C.G. Hanzlicek
1987
Some Gangster Pain, Gillian Conoley
Other Children, Lawrence Raab
Internal Geography, Richard Harteis
The Van Gogh Notebook, Peter Cooley
A Circus of Needs, Stephen Dunn (2nd edition)
Ruined Cities, Vern Rutsala
Places and Stories, Kim R. Stafford
1988
Preparing to Be Happy, T. Alan Broughton
Red Letter Days, Mekeel McBride
The Abandoned Country, Thomas Rabbitt
The Book of Knowledge, Dara Wier
Changing the Name to Ochester, Ed Ochester
Weaving the Sheets, Judith Root
1989
Recital in a Private Home, Eve Shelnutt
A Walled Garden, Michael Cuddihy
The Age of Krypton, Carol J. Pierman
Land That Wasn't Ours, David Keller
Stations, Jay Meek
The Common Summer: New and Selected Poems, Robert Wallace
The Burden Lifters, Michael Waters
Falling Deeply into America, Gregory Djanikian
Entry in an Unknown Hand, Franz Wright
1990
Why the River Disappears, Marcia Southwick
Staying Up For Love, Leslie Adrienne Miller
Dreamer, Primus St. John